Love Letters

Love

Love Letters

Sharon Luzzi

Copyright

Copyright © 2016 by Sharon Luzzi. All rights reserved. This book or any portion thereof may not be reproduced or used in any manner whatsoever without the express written permission of The Butterfly Typeface Publishing House Co. except for the use of brief quotations in a book review.

Scripture quotations are from The Holy Bible, English Standard Version® (ESV®), copyright © 2001 by Crossway, a publishing ministry of Good News Publishers. Used by permission. All rights reserved.

Printed in the United States of America

First Printing, 2016

ISBN-13: 978-1-942022-58-9

The Butterfly Typeface Publishing
PO BOX 56193
Little Rock, Arkansas 72215

Dedication

As I penned this from the Lord, I knew this for all those who are brokenhearted in the world and who need his healing peace.

So, for all of you who need Him, I dedicate this for your restoration and wholeness that only he can bring:

Isaiah 61

The Year of the Lord's Favor

1 The Spirit of the Lord God is upon me,
because the Lord has anointed me to
bring good news to the poor; he has sent
me to bind up the brokenhearted, to
proclaim liberty to the captives,
and the opening of the prison to those
who are bound;
2 to proclaim the year of the Lord's favor,
and the day of vengeance of our God;
to comfort all who mourn;
3 to grant to those who mourn in Zion—
to give them a beautiful headdress
instead of ashes, the oil of gladness
instead of mourning, the garment of
praise instead of a faint spirit; that they
may be called oaks of righteousness,
the planting of the Lord, that he may be
glorified.

4 They shall build up the ancient ruins; they shall raise up the former devastations; they shall repair the ruined cities, the devastations of many generations.
5 Strangers shall stand and tend your flocks; foreigners shall be your plowmen and vinedressers;
6 but you shall be called the priests of the Lord; they shall speak of you as the ministers of our God; you shall eat the wealth of the nations, and in their glory, you shall boast.
7 Instead of your shame there shall be a double portion; instead of dishonor they shall rejoice in their lot; therefore in their land they shall possess a double portion; they shall have everlasting joy.
8 For I the Lord love justice; I hate robbery and wrong; I will faithfully give them their recompense, and I will make an everlasting covenant with them.
9 Their offspring shall be known among the nations, and their descendants in the midst of the peoples; all who see them

shall acknowledge them, that they are an offspring the Lord has blessed.
10 I will greatly rejoice in the Lord; my soul shall exult in my God, for he has clothed me with the garments of salvation; he has covered me with the robe of righteousness, as a bridegroom decks himself like a priest with a beautiful headdress, and as a bride adorns herself with her jewels.
11 For as the earth brings forth its sprouts, and as a garden causes what is sown in it to sprout up, so the Lord God will cause righteousness and praise to sprout up before all the nations.

"Lies die hard, but the truth lives forever."

~ Sharon Luzzi

Table of Contents

Introduction 25
Love Letter One 27
Love Letter Two 29
Love Letter Three 39
Love Letter Four 41
Love Letter Five 47
Love Letter Six 49
Love Letter Seven 53
Love Letter Eight 55
Love Letter Nine 56
Love Letter Ten 57
Love Letter Eleven 59
Love Letter Twelve 63
Love Letter Thirteen 65
Love Letter Fourteen 69
Conclusion 71
About The Author 73

Foreword

Praise the Lord!

Our soul needs watering, kindness and soothing from the cares of daily life. As we take in the twist, turns, ups, the downs, and all the things that take away from our peace.

We need our souls watered, soothed, kindness and most of all, Love applied in all the right places.

We need refreshing and nourishment to keep our hearts full of Love and steady for the world we live in.

We need to be able to keep our hearts strong and to be able to pour into others. After ourselves, we need to pour into our families, neighbors and friends respectively.

The following Love Letters are to replenish and water your soul.

Who Is like the Lord Our God?

Psalm 113

1 Praise the Lord!
Praise, O servants of the Lord,
praise the name of the Lord!
2 Blessed be the name of the Lord
from this time forth and forevermore!
3 From the rising of the sun to its setting,
the name of the Lord is to be praised!
4 The Lord is high above all nations,
and his glory above the heavens!
5 Who is like the Lord our God,
who is seated on high,
6 who looks far down
on the heavens and the earth?
7 He raises the poor from the dust
and lifts the needy from the ash heap,
8 to make them sit with princes, with the
princes of his people.
9 He gives the barren woman a home
making her the joyous mother of children.

My Soul Thirsts for You

A Psalm of David, when he was in the wilderness of Judah.

1 O God, you are my God; earnestly I seek you;
my soul thirsts for you;
my flesh faints for you,
as in a dry and weary land where there is no water.
2 So I have looked upon you in the sanctuary,
beholding your power and glory.
3 Because your steadfast love is better than life,
my lips will praise you.
4 So I will bless you as long as I live;
in your name I will lift up my hands.
5 My soul will be satisfied as with fat and rich food, and my mouth will praise you with joyful lips,

6 when I remember you upon my bed,
and meditate on you in the watches of the night;
7 for you have been my help,
and in the shadow of your wings I will sing for joy.
8 My soul clings to you;
your right hand upholds me.
9 But those who seek to destroy my life
shall go down into the depths of the earth;
10 they shall be given over to the power of the sword;
they shall be a portion for jackals.
11 But the king shall rejoice in God;
all who swear by him shall exult,
for the mouths of liars will be stopped.

Acknowledgement

God is always number one in my mind for encouragement through his word.

I would like to thank all the many people who God sent along this crazy journey called life, too many to
name. They were always sent at the right moment for every little thing that I was struggling with to the biggest things that were beyond human understanding.

We still need each other.

I often had looked back thinking I was in dire need of this encouragement. Although, I could honestly say, I don't know how I got through it all without God.

It certainly was not by my own strength.

The people He sent were custom made for *each and every* moment and for each situation for the long haul.

I am so grateful and humbled.

From the bottom of my heart,

THANK YOU!

Introduction

These are a collection of Love Letters to fill you up with God's Love. To encourage you and stimulate your heart for Love and to Love.

They are from His heart to your heart.

They will help you look up!

They will restore, reassure, comfort and gladden your heart as you take in each word.

My greatest desire is to see you drawn closer to your Father's heart as you read this collection.

Love Letter One

my need for you is so great, father
i don't know what to ask
your people need and don't know how to ask or
what to ask
what do we ask?

i need **your wisdom, father**
i need your eyes to see
i need your ears to hear
i need your heart to know
i need you...

i need your love to melt the nations
i need your love to seek your peace
i need your peace

i need your heart to see the way you do
i need your heart to feed the nations
i need your heart to love
i need you...

i need your voice to proclaim the truth
i need your eyes to see the future
i need your ears to hear the pain

i need **your feet to crush my enemies**

i need **your heart to know you**
i need **your songs to break the atmosphere**
i need **your songs to soothe my soul**
i need **your heart to fill my lungs with your presence**

i need **your heart to feed your people**
i need **your spirit to make my way**
i need **your spirit to fill in the blanks**
i need **your spirit to see your ways**

i need **you in every special way**
i need **you…**

Love Letter Two

my people come sit at my feet so i can instruct you
come sit with me

do not tarry over there any longer
come here, come closer

do not delay in coming here
come sit with me
come sit with me
come now; with me
come delight with me
come be with me

do not second-guess, come sit with me
come know me
come hear me
come see me
come watch with me

come look into the long distance with me
come gaze with me
come love with me
come sit and create with me
come sit and sing with me

come sing to me

come inhabit the praises
come be intimate with me
come be sanctified
come be mine
come acknowledge me as king

king of your life
come my sons and daughters come be with me
for i am madly in love with you…
for these are the times i wait for

these are the days i wait for
come let me stroke your hair
let me stroke your head
come let me comfort you

come be mine
i have waited for a time like this
come i am waiting for you
i want to spend time with you

come there is no better time than now
come let me be frank and honest,
i want to spend time with you
come let me spend time with you

come let the door of your heart open to me
i am knocking on the door of your heart
come open the gates of your heart
come let me open the gates of your heart

Sharon Luzzi

i want to come in and sup with you
come let me heal the wounds
come let me speed up the recovery time
come let me cut away the deadness

come let me cut out the gangrene
come let me repair the holes left by battle
come let me in to restore your heart
from stone to flesh

come let me pour in love to displace the fear
come let me tear down the walls that keep me out
come let me prepare your heart
come let me make a way for you to come out of the darkness

come let me pour my liquid gold love
into those areas that just can't seem to be healed
come let me pour in the fragrance
that only i can bestow

come let me rain the fresh rain
into your thirsty spirit
come let me fill you up
with quenchable love

come let me enter in those places
that no one can enter
come let me fill up the gaps

Love Letters

that let things seep out
come let me fill up the places
that are rough and forbidding
come let me into the smallest place
that no one can see

come let me into the scary places
that you do not want anyone to know about

things in the past; things in the now
things you aren't sure how they got there
things of the obvious
things around
things behind
things deep in your heart that no one else knows
things that are in abundance; things that are not

things in that are in the forefront of your heart
things that are in hiding
things that are in the cracks and crevices
things in your heart that are longing
things in your heart that are missing
things that are; nonchalant and casual
things in your heart that have meaning

let me fill the places
that are bland
let me fill the places
that are old and dead

places that are bound
places that are dying
places that need renewing
places that need restoration
places that are absent of me
places that are unsure
places that are unsteady

places that need reassuring
places that are out of tune
places that are in tune
places that are dry
places that are jagged
places that are not, full of me
places that need intimacy

places that need jars full of clay
places that are unwitting
places of somberness
places of destitute
places of being surrounded

places in your heart that you need me
places that are long forgotten
places that need surrender
places that are aching
places that need honor
places that are harmed
places that are harmful

places that are acid
places that need neutralizing
places that have unfavorable conditions
places that need new life
places of observation
places of destruction

places in your heart that are under reconstruction
places of unfavorable conditions
places of condemnation
places of insurrection
places of disobedience
places in harm's way

places needing boundaries
places that abound
places that are longing for me
places only in your heart only i can see
only places i know about
places of unsure, unknowing, unbelief and instability

places of insecurity
places of wandering
places in the limelight
places of your contemporaries
places of not knowing, not knowing me, not knowing what to do
places of needing help but not wanting to ask

places only known to me
places of many faces
places of continuing pain

lingering thoughts
thoughts uncontrolled
thoughts raging
thoughts racing
thoughts of horror
thoughts of fear

come let me pour in my LOVE
let me pour in my everlasting love

LOVE beyond measure
LOVE beyond depth or width
LOVE that is unconditional
LOVE outstanding
LOVE outlasting
LOVE above all else
LOVE constrains

LOVE fulfills
LOVE that is faithful
LOVE that emits light
LOVE that is boundaries
LOVE that is bountiful
LOVE that never ends
LOVE unending

LOVE that is all things
LOVE that can't react but respond
LOVE that is sensitive and kind
LOVE that hears
hears the heart
LOVE that can't be measured by the world's standards

LOVE that is witty and light
LOVE without restrictions or ties
LOVE that says "can"
LOVE outstanding above all else
LOVE celebrated not fabricated
LOVE in action
LOVE overall

LOVE motivated by the heart of hearts
the king of kings
LOVE understanding and can function
LOVE captivating and empowering
LOVE with fire and passion
LOVE to supersede all human ideas
LOVE intensified

LOVE with no walls
LOVE without prejudice
LOVE not arranged or predisposed
LOVE that is open
LOVE that is healing
LOVE that is gracious

Sharon Luzzi

LOVE that is disarming
LOVE that is a hot flame

a burning flame laced with passion
a burning flame that is not reduced to favoritism

LOVE that spans all people
LOVE that spans all nations
LOVE that is full and fulfilling
LOVE that does not require
LOVE that does not expect back
LOVE that is full of expectancy
LOVE that gives hope and promise

LOVE that is to be trusted
LOVE that is committed and sure
LOVE that is honorable
LOVE that can see thru all things
LOVE that is surefooted
LOVE that is not ceremonious
LOVE that is simple and simplicity

LOVE that can't be denied
or swept under the carpet
LOVE of my making
LOVE in my name
LOVE for many
LOVE to die for
it was died for
it was given freely

Love Letters

Sharon Luzzi

Love

Sharon Luzzi

Love Letter Three

come drink from the wells of salvation

come drink freely

come drink freely

come my bride

come

come drink freely

come sit with me

come i call you by name

come

Sharon Luzzi

Love

Love Letter Four

my children much is coming
come to me for safety

come to me for protection
come, come, come under my wings
so i can cover you

come while the devastation passes
come know me come know my ways

know the course i have for you
do not despair for i am with you

let my river flow over you
come into the river

come there are deep oceans too
come in while you can

spend your time in worship
spend your time with me

come in for refreshing
come in for solvency

come stay with me for a while, come stay
come sit in my presence
come sit with me.
come worship me for worship is warfare

it is everything the enemy hates
come, you took his place

you are my worshippers extraordinaire
come worship me

you were created to worship
you were created with all the tools to worship

come i am calling you forth for such a time as this
come worship

come spend your quiet time with me
do not be distracted by the world

do not be distracted in these last days
these days that are, dark

do not be distracted by the terror that is going on
do not be distracted by unseen threats

do not be distracted by those things
that are not of me
do not be distracted by those things of darkness

do not be distracted by things of the world
do not be led astray
by the world and all that it holds

i did not create of that which is of man
come i am glory, not earthly things

i did not create chaos and fear on the earth
come press into me

come seek my heart to see who you are
do not let the world tell you who you are

you are my children
whom i have created for my purposes
you were not created for the purposes of the world

i am soon bringing my people out of Egypt, out of bondage

i am calling my people out of the world system
out of bondage

i am calling you out of bondage
calling you out of self-imposed slavery into this world system

come out!
come out!
come out!

do not stay!
it is only death

there is no life in the ways of man
my ways are not your ways

the world system is not of my making
think bigger!

think outside the world system
my kingdom is not fashioned
after the hand of man

it is not fashioned after human thinking
it is not fashioned in the traditions of man

do not conform to the ways of the world
do not follow the traditions of men

come follow my ways
learn my ways

look and believe
hear and believe
see and believe
know my ways
believe…

unbelief leads to hardness of heart
hardness of heart leads to falling away from me

Sharon Luzzi

believe my word

come eat of it
come dine with me
come break bread with me
come rest in me

Sharon Luzzi

Love

Sharon Luzzi

Love Letter Five

lean not on your own understanding

come follow my lead

come follow my way

come follow me

do not look to the left or to the right

Sharon Luzzi

Love

Love Letters

Love Letter Six

let me in to the depths of your soul
come let me in
i will only come in as you let me in
i will come in with light, kindness and most of all...
LOVE

LOVE and grace
do not be bothered by what you do not have
i will give you the rest
come...LOVE and grace
i will come into the depths of your soul
with loving kindness

come loving kindness...
LOVE as liquid gold
fire, authority and loving kindness
let me fill your heart one place at a time
into the depths of the unknown places
that you have

places that are even hidden to you
places that are fragile
places that need to be bonded to me
places that are, forever more to be close to me
places that are in need of return to me

places that have curled up edges;
that need to be redirected
places that are, even unfamiliar to you
places of great sustain
some that are, of great disdain

come let me in to those places in your heart that
are weak and failing
weak and falling down
weak and torn apart
shredded...

shredded beyond recognition
shredded without form where gangrene has set in
where there is nothing left
unrecognizable...

without description
without an address or memory any longer
without a known name or definition
without a name to be called out to anymore

i gently ask to come
into those places in your heart
i gently nod to those places
i see them with clarity
there is nothing hidden from me

nothing i can't comprehend
nothing i don't understand

nothing i cannot imagine or know
nothing that is too hard
for i was there when those things occurred
i wait patiently
i am calling
i am calling
i am calling

answer and you won't be disappointed
you won't be alarmed
you won't be sorry
you won't be hurt

LOVE covers all things
LOVE is supreme
LOVE is conquering king over all
LOVE is pure manifestation of my glory
LOVE is undying
LOVE is forever

LOVE is easily maintained
LOVE is perfect... you are not perfect... only i am.

you are saved by grace through faith
you take on my image
like a mirror of my character...

LOVE

Sharon Luzzi

Love

Love Letter Seven

wealth is beyond the eye of the beholder
wealth is not resident in oneself

wealth is part of my glory
abundance part of my glory

man's wealth is not my wealth
they are not the same

what is in the world is not mine
my glory is with me

man-made wealth does not compare
man-made wealth is no comparison

what you see in the world is man made
it's not of me

man is only passing around what he has made
you cannot see my glory in what man has made

come i will show you my glory
what i have made

Sharon Luzzi

Love

Love Letter Eight

*there are rivers and streams
that you are not aware of*

*come search my heart out for these things
search out my heart for all things*

*things you knew not
things you knew not of*

*come rivers and streams you know not
come; come with me*

*come walk with me
come walk with me*

Love Letter Nine

come i will let you into
the chambers

the chambers of my heart

chambers that are, full of me

chambers with much

chambers of me

chambers without darkness

come, come into
the chambers of my heart

Love Letter Ten

my beloved children come,
come follow me
i have much to give you
and much for you to see

come present yourselves
as a holy and living sacrifice
you will not be
disappointed

come follow me
come follow me

do not follow the traditions of men
come follow my ways, my heart
come follow me
come follow me

my children there is much coming
there is much for you to be aware of and much for
you to be ready for

my children there is much danger coming
on the land you need to be ready for
come, much

Sharon Luzzi

Love Letters

Love Letter Eleven

my children,
come travel with me to the highest heights
come travel with me across the plains
come travel with me to the deserts and rivers
come to my deepest oceans
come travel with me

come into my heart
let me make you part of my heart
come sit in LOVE with me
come spend time with me
come spend time with me
come while i wash your heart clean

come while i speak volumes to you
come while i put LOVE into your heart
come while i give you abundant life
come while i speak oceans to you
come do not delay i have much to give you
time is of the essence

come i will give you dreams and visions
come your destiny is at hand
come your destiny is at hand
come, come walk into your destiny

*come walk with me my children
come up here to the highest heights
come my children,
come with me into the sanctuary
come into the sanctuary
come walk with me into the meadows
the grasslands, deserts, the mountains, the plains,
the valleys, the rivers, the oceans, the lakes*

*come follow me
come follow me
come my children come follow me
my children i LOVE you deeper than you can imagine
come deeper than you can imagine*

*come follow me
come follow me into eternity
come follow me into your destiny
come be mine
let your destiny be my will for your life
come seek me for your life with me*

*come let me wash you, from the ways of the world
come let me relieve you, from the dust of the earth
let me fill you with my LOVE
come let me speak
into your wounded heart
and dispel the darkness*

come let me put light on the path
you are to follow
come let me put light in your life
come let me put light on your world for your
custom identity straight out of heaven
to you for you

come let me quantify who you are
come let me make you in my mirror image
come let me seal you in my LOVE
come let me into your heart
come let me instill in you, life……
come let me explain my mysteries

come let me judge your heart
come let me transfer all that i am to you
and for you
come do not despair
at what you know or don't know
come let me make you into my image

that's what salvation is
salvation is losing human knowing and gaining
who i am
come let me explain my mysteries to you
come let me show you my kingdom
come let me show you who i am

come know me
come know my ways
seek my ways
seek my face
come seek my kingdom and my righteousness
come seek all that i am

come seek me in the throne room
come seek me above all else
come seek me
come seek me
come seek me in the present
come seek me at night

come seek me during the day
come seek me all the time
come seek me in the early morning
when the dew is present
seek me when any condition is present

come my children i have much to tell you
come my children i LOVE you very much

Love Letter Twelve

let your scents be liken to mine
let your aroma be my perfume

let your essence be mine
come let your essence be mine

come let your embodiment be of me
let your whole person be of me

let your eyes sparkle into the galaxies and
heavenly realms
let your heart personify me

come let me heal you so i can present you
to the world, come let me present my bride

come let me present the sons and daughters
of the living god

come do not be afraid to let me into your heart
come let me enter into your heart

come let me shape you
and mold you into my image

not into the image man has created
not the image that man has defined
man cannot define me
only i can put you in my image

only i can put in you the structure
that i am

not man, man is limited
man is limited

man cannot create in you my character
man is shortsighted

man is dark
man can't bestow the beauty that i have

man is a vessel that can only contain
a limited amount of knowledge

man is limited
man is imperfect and fallen

my children the choice is always yours
your choice, which way you go

come you have been created with a free will

Love Letter Thirteen

my people i have been
languishing over you
i have come to take my people home
home where i will rule and reign

come i am long suffering over you
i am waiting with unparalleled pain
come i am waiting
for my bride to come back to me

come the wedding feast is prepared
a feast of reunion and reconnection
to my people;
whom i divorced long ago

come, my people whom i have come for
my people who i have
i long awaited for to come back
to me and my ways

come, my people i am waiting with open arms
my anger is no longer
my heart is toward you
now and forever

Sharon Luzzi

my LOVE is an everlasting LOVE
my LOVE is long and deep and broad
come an everlasting LOVE
come, come sit with me at the banqueting table
at the wedding feast
come i am waiting
for my people to reunite with me

a long time has gone by
and i have never forsaken you
or forgotten you
i have never come empty handed

come my children i am waiting
i have abundance and newness
i have greatness and freshness
fresh oil and gladness and joy and an open heart...

the heart of god
is no longer closed off to his people
come the flood gates are open
come i long to spend time with you

i long to be close to you
i long to hear you calling
me by my name
i long to hear your heart toward mine

i long to hear your story
i long to hear you

Sharon Luzzi

*my children we have entered into
a new part of relationship*

*come seek me
come seek me
come i hear you and i see you
come my children*

come

Sharon Luzzi

Love

Love Letter Fourteen

let me in to the depths of your soul
come let me in
i will only come in as you let me in

i will come in with light, kindness and most of all
...LOVE,
LOVE and grace

do not be bothered by what you do not have
i will give you the rest
come...LOVE and grace

i will come into the depths of your soul
with loving kindness
come loving kindness...

LOVE as liquid gold
fire, authority and loving kindness
let me fill your heart one place at a time

into the depths
of the unknown places
that you have

places that are even hidden to you

*places that are fragile
places that need to be bonded to me
places that are, forever more
to be close to me
places that are in need of return to me*

*places that have curled up edges;
that need to be redirected
places that are, even unfamiliar to you*

*places of great sustain
some that are
of great disdain*

*come let me in to those places
in your heart that are weak and failing
weak and falling down; weak and torn apart*

*shredded...
shredded beyond recognition
shredded without form where gangrene has set in*

*where there is nothing left
unrecognizable...*

Conclusion

Our Messiah came to teach His people how to walk in LOVE. He was the greatest example that we could have to learn how to LOVE.

He was misunderstood, unrecognized, forsaken, and most of all misrepresented.

His presence will be felt all over the earth and the manifestation of His Glory will be seen.

This is the greatest time in history to accept these
healing words into your heart.

And the greatest of these is LOVE...

The only force that will heal all peoples, all nations and all tongues:

Love

About the Author

Sharon Luzzi is a mom, (meemaw) grandma, (gramio) and a forerunner/visionary in many arenas.

She has been involved in her community, church, and regional politics.

Her desire is to encourage, empower and transform people through God's word and the wisdom that comes with it.

Her interests range from writing, painting, photography, writing songs and creating to riding horses, spending time at the beach and finding out about the latest formula 500 car.

However, what Sharon loves most is spending time with her family.

The Butterfly Typeface Publishing House Co.

The Butterfly Typeface Publishing House Company is a full service professional publishing company. Our goal is to 'spread a message' of inspiration, imagination and intrigue in all that we do.

Whether you hire us to edit, ghostwrite, publish (books & magazines) or web design, you can be guaranteed exemplary customer service, fairness and quality.

Our vision, under God's leadership, is to serve and assist in the healing of the heart, mind and soul of *all* people we encounter with integrity, intentional influence and positive purpose.

"We make good GREAT!"

Iris M. Williams – Owner
The Butterfly Typeface Publishing House Co
Little Rock Arkansas

www.butterflytypeface.com

www.ingramcontent.com/pod-product-compliance
Lightning Source LLC
Chambersburg PA
CBHW061508040426
42450CB00008B/1527